➤A STEP INTO HISTORY™➤

WORLD WAR II

BY STEVEN OTFINOSKI

Series Editor
Elliott Rebhun, Editor & Publisher,
The New York Times Upfront
at Scholastic

■SCHOLASTIC

Content Consultant: James Marten, PhD, Professor and Chair, History
Department, Marquette University, Milwaukee, Wisconsin

Cover: Allied soldiers wade through the water during World War II.

Library of Congress Cataloging-in-Publication Data
Names: Otfinoski, Steven, author.
Title: World War II / by Steven Otfinoski.
Other titles: World War Two
Description: New York, NY : Children's Press, an imprint of Scholastic, 2017.
    | Series: A Step into history | Includes index.
Identifiers: LCCN 2016030826| ISBN 9780531225721 (library binding) |
    ISBN 9780531243664 (pbk.)
Subjects: LCSH: World War, 1939-1945—Juvenile literature.
Classification: LCC D743.7 .O73 2017 | DDC 940.53—dc23
LC record available at https://lccn.loc.gov/2016030826

All rights reserved. Published in 2017 by Children's Press, an imprint of
Scholastic Inc. Published simultaneously in Canada. Printed in Malaysia 108

1 2 3 4 5 6 7 8 9 10 R 26 25 24 23 22 21 20 19 18 17

CONTENTS

PROLOGUE

IN 1918, WORLD WAR I ENDED WITH THE DEFEAT of Germany and Austria-Hungary at the hand of the Allies, including the United States. The Allies forced Germany to give up territory and most of its military. Germany also had to pay an enormous amount of money for the costs of war and was left broken and humiliated.

In 1929, the Great Depression put millions of people across the globe out of work. Germany was hit hard, and it turned to a new leader who promised to make the country great again. His name was Adolf Hitler, and his Nazi Party grew in strength as more Germans became dissatisfied with their government. Once in power, Hitler not only built up Germany's economy, but also its military. European nations like France and Great Britain realized Hitler was preparing for war, but failed to stop him.

In September 1939, World War II erupted, setting Germany and its allies, Japan and Italy (the Axis powers), against most of the rest of Europe (the Allies). While Hitler craved conquest, he also sought revenge on an entire people—the Jews of Europe. In his twisted mind, he saw Jews as responsible for Germany's problems and set out

to eliminate them. Hitler's brutal murder of six
million Jews and other people has come to be called
the Holocaust.

In December 1941, the United States entered
the war to defeat the Axis powers. It helped lead
the Allies to victory, but at a terrible price.

When the war ended in August 1945, it had
brought even greater death and destruction than
World War I.

A World War II bomber plane

THE TWO SIDES IN WORLD WAR II

THE ALLIES

GREAT BRITAIN
(September 3, 1939)

Dates in parentheses show when each country entered the war.

FRANCE
(September 3, 1939)

AUSTRALIA
(September 3, 1939)

CANADA
(September 10, 1939)

The Soviet Union and Germany had signed a pact in 1939 to not fight each other, but the Soviets joined the Allies after Germany invaded the Soviet Union in 1941.

GREECE
(October 28, 1940)

SOVIET UNION
(June 22, 1941)

UNITED STATES
(December 8, 1941)

CHINA
(December 8, 1941)

China joined the Allies in 1941, but had been fighting Japan since 1937.

THE AXIS POWERS

GERMANY
(September 1, 1939)

ITALY
(June 11, 1940)

JAPAN
(September 27, 1940)

HUNGARY
(November 20, 1940)

ROMANIA
(November 23, 1940)

BULGARIA
(March 1, 1943)

MAPS

EUROPE IN 1942

By 1942, Germany and the other Axis powers
had expanded their territory to include
much of Europe and parts of Africa.

Axis countries

Axis-controlled or
occupied territories

Allied countries

Neutral countries or
territories

☆ Major battle

Scale:
0 — 200 MI
0 — 400 KM

ICELAND
Reykjavík

ATLANTIC
OCEAN

NORWAY
Oslo

SWEDEN

FINLAND
Helsinki

Estonia

North
Sea

DENMARK

Baltic
Sea

Latvia

Moscow

Lithuania

IRELAND

GREAT
BRITAIN

NETHERLANDS
Copenhagen

East
Prussia

SOVIET UNION

London

Berlin

BELGIUM

GERMANY

POLAND
Sudetenland

English Channel

Normandy

Paris

LUX.

Nuremberg

Prague
CZECHOSLOVAKIA

EUROPE

Stalingrad

LIECH.

Vienna

Budapest

FRANCE

SWITZ.

AUSTRIA

HUNGARY

ROMANIA

Black Sea

Belgrade

Bucharest

PORTUGAL

ITALY

YUGOSLAVIA

BULGARIA

ANDORRA

Corsica

Rome

Sofia

Istanbul

N

SPAIN

ALBANIA

T U R K E Y

W   E

Sardinia

GREECE

S

Mediterranean Sea

Sicily

Athens

CYPRUS
(BRITAIN)

AFRICA

MALTA

THE PACIFIC IN 1942

The area around the Pacific Ocean played a very important role in World War II. Japan had been expanding its territory since 1931, beginning with the invasion of Manchuria.

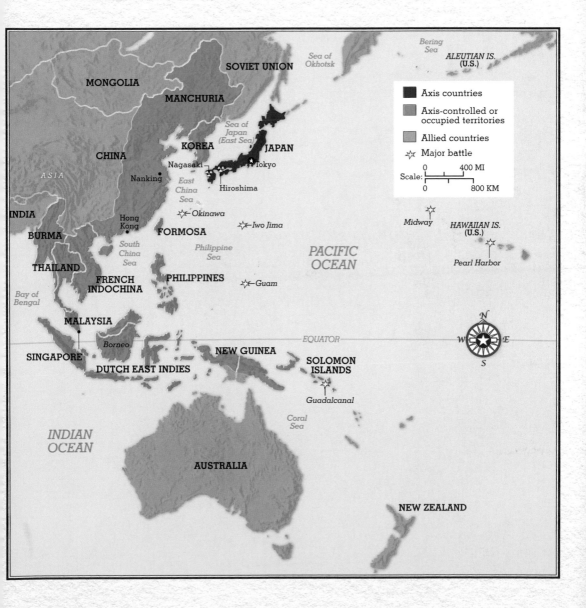

66 *Strength lies not in defense but in attack.* 99

—ADOLF HITLER

CHAPTER 1

DAY OF THE DICTATORS

Europe was devastated after World War I ended in 1918. People looked to strong leaders to rebuild their countries from the ruins of the war.

You will find the definitions of bold words in the glossary on pages 140–41.

THE 1920S WERE A TIME OF HARDSHIP and struggle in Europe. Both the winners and losers of World War I (1914–18) suffered in the war's aftermath. Many people sought leaders who promised to make their countries strong and powerful again. In Italy, Benito Mussolini founded the country's **Fascist** Party in 1919. A year later, **Adolf Hitler** joined the Nazi Party in Germany.

By the 1930s, both Mussolini and Hitler had gained the support of many people and become **dictators** in their countries. In Japan, General **Hideki Tojo** gained power. These men silenced all political opposition and ruled with an iron hand. They built up their countries' economies and strengthened their military might. They sought to conquer other nations and create empires in Europe, Asia, and Africa. To this end, Japan invaded and occupied the Chinese province of Manchuria in 1931, and Italy invaded the African country of Ethiopia in 1935. The day of the dictators had begun.

Find out more about people whose names appear in orange and bold on pages 136–37.

Italian dictator Benito Mussolini (left) meets with Adolf Hitler (right) during a 1937 visit to Germany.

Mussolini's "Roman salute" was a symbol of facism in Italy. The salute was also adopted by the Nazis.

The swastika was one of the main symbols of the Nazi Party.

LV

CHAPTER 2

BLITZKRIEG!

Hitler wanted to conquer all of Europe.
Everyone wondered where he would strike first.

IN 1936, HITLER SENT TROOPS INTO THE Rhineland, a part of Germany that had been made a **demilitarized** zone after World War I. This was a violation of the Treaty of Versailles, which Germany had signed after the war. France and Great Britain could have stepped in, but they were reluctant to risk another war. Instead, they pursued a policy of **appeasement**, believing that Hitler would not further violate the treaty. However, Hitler marched into neighboring Austria in 1938. Some Austrians welcomed him as a hero. Many of them had German roots and hoped unification with Germany would improve their lives. Then Hitler seized the Sudetenland, a region of Czechoslovakia populated largely by Germans.

In March 1939, German troops took the rest of Czechoslovakia. Finally, on September 1, 1939, Germany attacked Poland. As German planes destroyed the Polish air force on the ground and then bombed its cities, army divisions advanced into the countryside. The Germans called this fast-paced style of war *blitzkrieg*, or "lightning war." Great Britain and France could no longer ignore Hitler's aggression. Two days after the invasion of Poland, both countries declared war on Germany.

German soldiers form a motorcycle convoy in Berlin before invading Poland in 1939.

President Franklin D. Roosevelt
addresses the nation on the radio
in September 1939 to declare U.S.
neutrality at the start of World War II.

CHAPTER 3

AMERICA ON THE SIDELINES

Europe was at war, and many people wondered
if the United States would join the conflict.

Hitler was often called the Führer (German for "leader").

BY MAY 1940, HITLER'S WAR MACHINE was rolling across Europe. One by one, Denmark, Norway, Belgium, Luxembourg, and the Netherlands fell to the German blitzkrieg. American leaders watched the war with growing concern, but avoided joining in. **Isolationists** in Congress did not want to see the United States involved in another foreign war like World War I. Other Americans wanted to see the Allies (France and Great Britain) win, but preferred to remain **neutral**. Still others wanted the United States to more actively support the Allies with money and supplies.

President Franklin D. Roosevelt felt deeply that the Allies should be supported. He began sending aid in the form of money and **armaments**, but continued to keep the United States out of direct conflict. At the same time, he pursued a policy of preparedness, building up the military by calling the National Guard into service in case the United States was forced to join the conflict.

In 1939, a worker at the U.S. Senate post office sorts through a huge amount of mail from citizens with opinions on the war.

JUNE 22
*France surrenders
to Germany.*

 1940 JAN FEB MAR APR MAY JUN JUL AUG SEP OCT NOV

CHAPTER 4

THE FALL OF FRANCE

France felt safe from a German invasion. However, this sense of safety soon proved misguided.

THOUGH THEY WATCHED THEIR NEIGHBORS fall to Hitler's blitzkrieg, most people in France felt safe. They were confident that the Maginot Line—a series of underground fortresses that formed a line of defense along France's eastern border—would keep the Germans out. However, these defenses were not as strong as the French thought. The Germans simply crossed through Belgium *north* of the Maginot Line in June 1940. They quickly defeated the French forces. Around this time, Italy joined into an **alliance** with Germany, forming the Axis powers. As Germany attacked in the north of France, Italy attacked in the south.

On June 14, German troops marched into Paris, passing through the Arc de Triomphe, a symbol of French pride, as thousands of French citizens watched and wept. The French government fled to the south and the new French leader, Henri-Philippe Petain, signed an **armistice** with the Germans. The armistice signing took place on June 22, in a railway coach at Compiegne—the exact place Germany had surrendered to France in World War I on November 11, 1918.

Paris was taken without a single shot being fired.

Hitler (second from right) marches in front of the Eiffel Tower in Paris, France, in 1940.

JULY

Germany begins a massive bombing campaign against Great Britain, with plans for a land invasion.

1940 JAN FEB MAR APR MAY JUN JUL AUG SEP OCT NOV

CHAPTER 5

THE BATTLE OF BRITAIN

With France's fall, Great Britain stood alone against the Axis powers. Its people prepared for the worst.

IN JULY 1940, THE GERMAN LUFTWAFFE BEGAN attacking Great Britain from the air. Hitler expected the bombs to quickly destroy the British Royal Air Force (RAF), paving the way for a land invasion of Britain called Operation Sea Lion. However, he didn't count on the grit and determination of the British people and their new prime minister, **Winston Churchill**.

The Luftwaffe hammered England for eight months. In the capital city of London, thousands of civilians were killed by bombs and many buildings and homes were destroyed. However, the Luftwaffe was eventually beaten back by RAF fighter squadrons, even though the British planes were outnumbered three to one.

On October 30, Hitler called off the bombing and abandoned Operation Sea Lion. In a tribute to the RAF pilots, Churchill said, "Never was so much owed by so many to so few."

A German plane flies above London, England, during the bombing campaign in 1940.

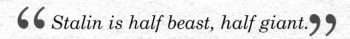 *Stalin is half beast, half giant.*

—Adolf Hitler, 1942

CHAPTER 6

HITLER AND STALIN

The Führer was not afraid to betray his
allies in his quest to conquer Europe.

The Soviet Union was officially called the Union of Soviet Socialist Republics (USSR). It included present-day Russia and many nearby countries.

JOSEPH STALIN, THE LEADER OF THE SOVIET Union, had formed a nonagression pact with Hitler in August 1939, shortly before Germany invaded Poland. The two allies divided Poland between themselves, the Germans taking the western half and Soviets taking the eastern half, as well as the Baltic states of Latvia, Lithuania, and Estonia. But Stalin was foolish to put his trust in a man as ruthless as Hitler. Betraying his ally's trust, Hitler sent three million German troops to attack the Soviet Union on June 22, 1941.

Stalin was caught entirely by surprise and went into a panic. He locked himself in a room and wasn't seen for four days. By June 30, several Soviet cities had fallen to the Germans. However, the Soviet people bravely fought back.

One arm of the German forces marched toward Moscow, the Soviet capital. By the time they reached the city's outskirts in late 1941, their forces had been critically depleted by the Soviets and the bitter cold. The Soviets counterattacked, forcing the Germans to retreat and ending Hitler's attempt to capture Moscow.

German tanks and machine gunners march through the trenches in the Soviet Union in December 1942.

Americans were shocked by news of the attack on Pearl Harbor in Hawaii.

CHAPTER 7

A DAY OF INFAMY

The United States had stayed out of the war for more than two years. But on a bright Sunday morning in December 1941, all that changed.

AMERICA'S RELATIONS WITH JAPAN HAD been tense since the Japanese invaded Manchuria, a Chinese province in northeastern Asia, in 1931. More recently, Japan had alarmed the United States by moving into Southeast Asia. President Roosevelt warned Japan to stay out of the region and began to prepare for the possibility of war.

That possibility became a certainty on the morning of December 7, 1941. Japanese bomber planes launched a surprise attack on the U.S. naval fleet in Pearl Harbor, Hawaii, catching the United States completely unaware. Black smoke and the smell of explosives filled the air as U.S. forces scrambled to mount a defense.

All of America was shattered by the news of the attack. The following day, President Roosevelt asked <u>Congress</u> for a declaration of war against Japan. He got his declaration and the solid support of the entire country. Those who had opposed going to war were now ready to seek revenge. Japan's allies, Germany and Italy, quickly declared war against the United States in response. It was now truly a world war.

The only "no" vote for war was cast by Rep. Jeannette Rankin of Montana, the first woman elected to Congress.

U.S. Navy soldiers stand among the wreckage during the attack on Pearl Harbor.

Within a few hours, Japan had sunk 18 U.S. ships and killed or wounded some 3,700 people in Pearl Harbor.

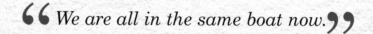

We are all in the same boat now.

—FRANKLIN ROOSEVELT TO
WINSTON CHURCHILL DURING
A PHONE CALL ON DECEMBER 7,
1941, THE DAY OF THE PEARL
HARBOR ATTACK

CHAPTER 8

ROOSEVELT AND CHURCHILL

The fate of the free world lay in the
hands of two powerful men.

CHURCHILL WAS SADDENED BY THE American losses, but glad that the United States was now in the war. Roosevelt and Churchill got along well and became fast friends, even though their personalities were very different. Roosevelt was more secretive and calculating. Churchill was more open, expressive, and emotional. The two leaders grew to appreciate each other's differences and worked together closely toward a common cause.

Churchill spent Christmas 1941 at the White House as Roosevelt's guest. The two men planned war strategy and thoroughly enjoyed each other's company. "They look like two little boys playing soldier," said Eleanor Roosevelt, the president's wife. Roosevelt and Churchill rarely disagreed.

The same could not be said for the other two leaders of the "Big Four" Allied powers, Stalin and Chiang Kai-shek of China—both of whom distrusted the Americans and the British.

President Roosevelt (left) and Prime Minister Churchill (right) meet onboard the British ship Prince of Wales *in August 1941.*

Because President Roosevelt wore metal braces to support his paralyzed legs, it is rare to see a photo of him from the waist down.

This internment camp in Amache, Colorado, was built to hold 7,000 Japanese Americans during the war.

CHAPTER 9

JAPANESE INTERNMENT CAMPS

American fears led to one of the darkest
periods in the nation's history.

JAPAN'S ATTACK ON PEARL HARBOR HAD severe repercussions for many Japanese Americans. A wave of anti-Japanese sentiment swept the country. Fearing that they might be spies for Japan, the U.S. government in early 1942 removed 110,000 Japanese Americans from their homes on the West Coast. They were imprisoned in quickly built internment camps on government lands, mostly in the deserts of California. Many of them lost their homes, businesses, and other valuable assets. The camps were crowded, with families often sharing one-room cells. The camps were encircled by barbed wire and patrolled by guards.

The detainees were not allowed to return to their homes until December 1944. There was no evidence that any of these people had ever been spies. Despite their treatment, many of the detainees were determined to show their loyalty to America. They enlisted in the armed forces and served with courage and distinction.

In 1988, President Ronald Reagan signed the Civil Liberties Act that gave a formal apology and $20,000 in compensation to each survivor of the internment camps.

Ten Americans were eventually convicted of spying for Japan, but none were of Japanese ancestry.

Japanese Americans board trains to an internment camp in April 1942.

CHAPTER 10

THE DESERT FOX

The war brought the Allies into North Africa,
where they met a formidable enemy.

Both Italy and Great Britain
had colonies in North Africa.

IN 1940, ITALY LAUNCHED A CAMPAIGN AGAINST Great Britain in <u>North Africa</u>, further expanding the war. Mussolini's objective was Egypt, the key to the defense of the eastern Mediterranean region. When Italian troops faltered before a British counterattack, Hitler sent in troops to aid his ally. They were led by Field Marshal Erwin Rommel.

Rommel's <u>clever tactics</u> in fighting the Allies in North Africa earned him the nickname the Desert Fox. Despite his skills, on October 23, 1942, Rommel—short on troops and supplies—suffered a devastating defeat at the Battle of El Alamein in Egypt when British commander General Bernard L. Montgomery attacked with tanks and infantry. North Africa was saved from the Axis forces.

Rommel continued to fight for his country, despite his growing belief that Germany could not win the war. He was later implicated, probably falsely, in a plot to kill Hitler and end the war. In 1944, Rommel used poison to kill himself rather than face a trial that could have put his family at risk.

The Germans buried 500,000 mines in the desert in a belt 40 miles (64.4 kilometers) long that Rommel called the Devil's Garden.

Field Marshal Rommel gives orders to his troops in North Africa in 1943.

*Resistance members gather in
secret to plan their operations
sometime during the war.*

CHAPTER 11

THE FRENCH RESISTANCE

France was under German control,
but that didn't stop some French men and
women from fighting for their country.

Other resistance movements formed in countries such as Poland, Greece, and the Netherlands.

THOUSANDS OF FRENCH MEN AND WOMEN were part of a secret underground movement called the <u>French Resistance</u>. They loved their country fiercely and did everything they could to thwart the German occupation. Resistance members sabotaged Nazi arms factories, blew up bridges, derailed trains, and cut telephone and telegraph lines. They also worked as spies and provided valuable intelligence about German troops and strategy to the Allies. If captured, Resistance members faced a quick end by firing squad, or, as in the case of Resistance leader Jean Moulin, were tortured to death.

By 1944, there were about 100,000 members of the French Resistance. About 10 percent of them were women. Some women worked as spies, and others fought alongside the men.

Despite the risks they faced, the members of the French Resistance hurt the Germans and helped strengthen the Allies' cause.

Resistance members protest German occupation by playing the French national anthem through loudspeakers in 1945.

Posters encouraged Americans to grow their own food during the war.

CHAPTER 12

AMERICA'S HOME FRONT

Americans back home did their part to win the war.

WHILE MILLIONS OF AMERICAN MEN and women fought the Axis powers in Europe and the Pacific, the American public did its part for the war effort at home. They took new jobs in **munitions** and aircraft factories and bought more than $180 billion in government war bonds, which were special funds the government used to pay for the war.

People grew their own vegetables in backyard "victory gardens" so farm crops could be sent to feed the troops. Children and adults showed their patriotism by holding drives to collect tin cans, wastepaper, and aluminum pots and pans—all used as <u>raw materials</u> to be recycled into war products.

Food and other goods were sent to feed and care for American soldiers, creating shortages at home. Everything from butter and meat to cars and gasoline were **rationed** because they were in short supply. That led to the development of a thriving **black market** for rationed goods.

Housewives even collected cooking grease for the army to use to make explosives.

Boys pose with the pile of scrap metal they collected during a "victory drive" in 1943.

GIVE IT YOUR BEST!

Factory workers assemble parts
for tanks and aircraft in the
United States in 1943.

CHAPTER 13

WOMEN IN THE WAR

American and British women found new purpose and independence in ways they couldn't have imagined before the war.

WITH SO MANY ABLE-BODIED MEN off to war, six million American women went to work outside their homes during the war, many for the first time. They were air-raid wardens in cities and Red Cross workers in hospitals after the attack on Pearl Harbor.

As the war continued, many took on jobs previously reserved for men. Women worked in munitions factories, aircraft plants, and shipyards. They were paid well for their work and were able to support their families. This gave them a sense of independence and self-worth many had never experienced before.

A number of women also went to war. Some 350,000 women enlisted in the armed services. They served as mechanics, clerks, and airfield control-tower operators. British women also went to work during the war. All British women between the ages of 18 and 60 were required to work at war-related jobs. Among them were thousands of young women who worked to decipher encoded messages sent between German generals. They had to keep their work secret, even from their families.

A woman works at an arms manufacturing plant in 1943.

"The American soldier is quick in adapting himself to a new mode of living."

—WAR JOURNALIST ERNIE PYLE

CHAPTER 14

G.I. JOE

Many of the American men who went off to war
didn't know what they were getting into.

THE AVERAGE AMERICAN INFANTRYMAN HAD no experience in war, didn't know how to shoot a gun, and hadn't ever traveled outside his home state. Unlike the volunteers in the navy and the Marine Corps, these raw army recruits were usually **drafted**. By 1942, the first year the United States was in the war, there were more than three million men in the army. Because their clothes and other belongings were "government issued" when they joined the army, they came to be called G.I.s.

G.I. Joe later became a popular soldier toy for several generations of children.

These young men learned about soldiering at training camps across the United States where tough-as-nails drill sergeants shouted orders at them. After months of training, they were sent abroad to fight in the Pacific, North Africa, or Great Britain.

Bored G.I.s spent the days and weeks between battles reading mail from home, playing cards, and complaining about the food (which was actually better than the meals fed to soldiers by many other nations). But when the time came for combat, they were as good as any other soldiers on the battlefield. They were there, as one reporter put it, to "get the job done."

U.S. Navy cadets climb a net during training in Corpus Christi, Texas, in 1942.

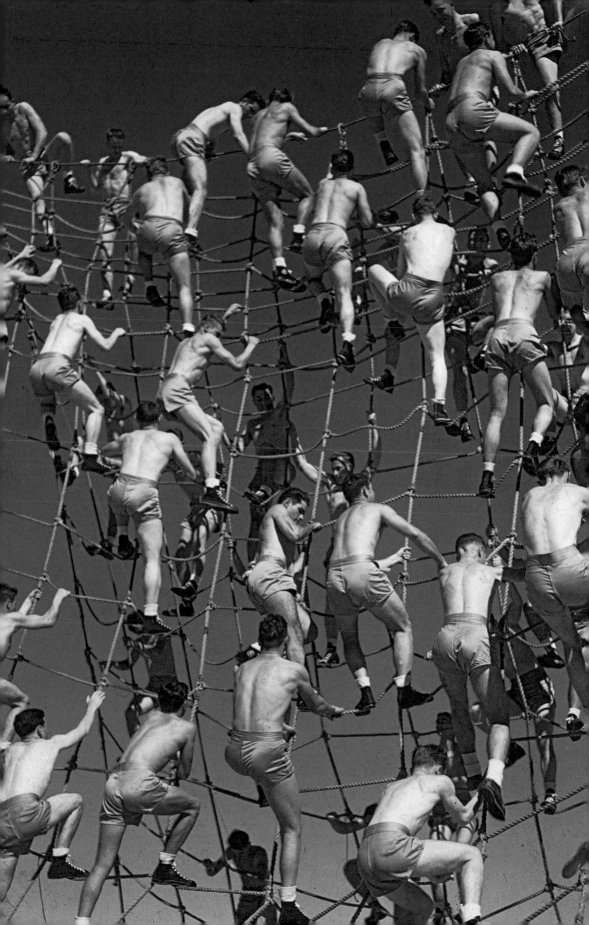

An army private dances with his date at a USO event in 1942.

CHAPTER 15

ENTERTAINING THE TROOPS

Amid the chaos of war, soldiers needed
a way to relax and unwind.

THOUSANDS OF MILES AWAY FROM HOME and family, many American soldiers felt lonely and homesick. Nothing made many of them happier than seeing a live stage show put on by the United Service Organizations (USO). Hollywood stars such as singer Bing Crosby, actress Marlene Dietrich, and actor Mickey Rooney were flown to every corner of the world where soldiers were stationed. Comedian Bob Hope was the star of many of these shows. His standard line to soldiers he visited in military hospitals always got a laugh: "Hi. Did you see my show tonight or were you already sick?"

When home in the states on leave, a brief period of rest from duty, soldiers looking for a fun night could visit a USO Stage Door Canteen in many big cities. There, they could eat, relax, dance, and see live entertainment, all for free. At the first Stage Door Canteen in New York City, a soldier might be surprised to see stage or movie stars serving him food or cleaning up tables, doing their part for the troops.

U.S. Navy sailors play pool at a USO facility in Trinidad.

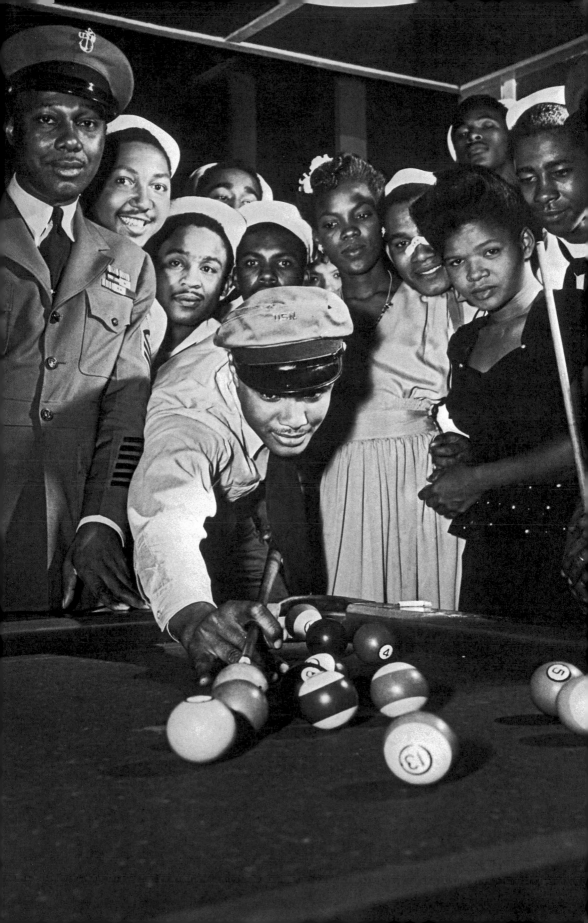

CHAPTER 16

THE HOLOCAUST

Hitler's hatred of the Jewish people led to one of the darkest events in human history.

DURING HIS RISE TO POWER IN THE 1920s, Hitler wrote and published a book called *Mein Kampf* (My Struggle). In it, he unfairly blamed many of Germany's problems on the Jewish people. By 1941, Hitler was ready to act on a plan known as the "final solution." Jews throughout German-controlled Europe were rounded up. Some were shot by firing squads. Others were forced out of their homes and into crowded neighborhoods called **ghettos**. Eventually, most were packed into train cars and sent to concentration camps located mainly in Germany and Poland. At these camps, Jews were killed in poison gas chambers. Others were put to work manufacturing supplies for the German military. Those who weren't gassed often died from overwork, starvation, or disease. Over four years, nearly six million Jews perished in the camps.

This systematic attempt to eliminate the Jewish people has come to be called the Holocaust. In addition to the Jewish victims, around three million other people died in the Holocaust, including Gypsies, people with disabilities, and homosexuals. Word of the camps leaked out to the Allies, but few people believed that even the Nazis could do such terrible things.

There is a Holocaust Memorial Museum in Washington, D.C. It has had more than 40 million visitors since it opened in 1993.

Jewish children stand behind barbed wire at the Auschwitz concentration camp in Poland in 1945.

A helmet and goggles used by British pilots in World War II

CHAPTER 17

THE BATTLE OF MIDWAY

The Japanese were bent on winning the
war in the Pacific, but the Americans
hoped to stop them at a small island.

AFTER THEIR SUCCESSFUL ATTACK ON Pearl Harbor, the Japanese began taking island after island in the Pacific. On June 4, 1942, a huge Japanese **armada** attacked American-held Midway Island, which lay 1,000 miles (1,609 km) from Hawaii. Its strategic position made it the key for Japanese control of the north Pacific.

The day before, Japanese planes had attacked Alaska's Aleutian Islands, hoping to distract the Americans from Midway. But the Americans were not fooled. They were ready at Midway, and their dive bombers sank four Japanese aircraft carriers. All four of the carriers had taken part in the attack on Pearl Harbor. It was a fitting act of revenge for that sneak attack six months earlier. The Japanese were soon in full retreat.

Midway was the first naval defeat ever for Japan and one of the most decisive battles of the war. While the Japanese did seize two of the Aleutian Islands, they were driven out in summer 1943. This was the only time during the war that North American territory was occupied by the enemy.

U.S. bomber planes patrol near Midway Island in 1942.

66 *I would rather fly . . . against the [Japanese] three times a day than fly a transport over the Hump once.* **99**

—U.S. FIGHTER PILOT
LIEUTENANT TOMMY HARMON

CHAPTER 18

THE HUMP AIRMEN

Not all American pilots saw combat. One
group of supply pilots faced some of the
greatest challenges of the war.

THE CHINA-BURMA-INDIA **THEATER** PLAYED an important role in World War II. When the Japanese seized Burma, an important land route from India to China was closed off. As a result, American planes carried <u>much-needed supplies</u> from India to China during the war.

The air route crossed the Himalayas, the world's highest mountain range. This was the "hump" that the American pilots had to get over. Many of them didn't make it and crashed in the snowy mountain peaks. Others lost their planes in Burma's jungles, where they struggled to survive after crashing. Brave Americans on search-and-rescue teams parachuted into the jungles to find these lost airmen and bring them to safety.

The "Hump airmen" played a critical role in defeating Japan. They helped the Chinese keep the Japanese at bay and forced Japan to send more soldiers into China, depleting the country's manpower in the Pacific theater.

During their three-year mission, the Hump airmen delivered more than 700,000 tons of supplies to the Chinese front.

U.S. paratroopers practice jumping from planes in 1943.

Paratroopers dropped to the ground from thousands of feet in the air.

JANUARY 31

The Soviets defeat
Germany at the Battle
of Stalingrad.

1943 JAN FEB MAR APR MAY JUN JUL AUG SEP OCT NOV

CHAPTER 19

THE BATTLE OF STALINGRAD

Hitler was ready to attack the Soviet Union again. His target was a city that was named after Stalin himself.

IN THE SUMMER OF 1942, HITLER SENT AN ARMY of more than 300,000 soldiers to take the Soviet industrial center of Stalingrad on the Volga River. German artillerymen soon reduced the city to rubble, but the Soviets held out and the **siege** went on for months.

The fighting was intense, with soldiers battling hand-to-hand amid the city's buildings. Sharp-eyed Soviet **snipers** picked off German soldiers from windows and foxholes and then moved on to new positions through underground tunnels. Finally, two Soviet armies arrived on the scene and surrounded the Germans.

When the weary, discouraged Germans surrendered on January 31, 1943, only 90,000 of the original force remained alive. It was the biggest defeat a German field army had ever experienced and a major turning point in the war.

Soviet soldiers fire from wrecked buildings during the Battle of Stalingrad in 1942.

Bugs Bunny was among the many popular characters to appear in anti-Axis cartoons during the war.

CHAPTER 20

CARTOONS GO TO WAR

The war was fought not only with bullets
but also with words and images.

IN THE 1940s, SHORT CARTOONS WERE OFTEN shown before the main feature film at movie theaters. Many cartoons produced during the war served as **propaganda**. They allowed Americans to laugh at the enemy and raised their spirits. Walt Disney won an Oscar for Best Animated Short in 1943 for *Der Fuehrer's Face*, a biting satire of German Führer (also spelled *Fuehrer*) Adolf Hitler. Warner Brothers' Looney Tunes cartoons sent Daffy Duck and Bugs Bunny to war in such animated shorts as *Draftee Daffy* and *Herr* (German for "mister") *Meets Hare*.

As with all war propaganda, these cartoons were meant to stir up people's emotions against the enemy. Their creators often relied on racial stereotypes to get a reaction from audiences.

One popular cartoon character during the war was Private Snafu, an unlucky American soldier. The mistakes made by Snafu were meant to instruct real soldiers on how to avoid making the same mistakes. In one cartoon, Snafu gossips about troop movements with an enemy spy and causes American forces to lose a battle.

One of the writers of the Private Snafu cartoons was Theodor Geisel, who would later become famous as Dr. Seuss.

A poster for Der Fuehrer's Face *shows Donald Duck attacking an image of Adolf Hitler.*

er Fuehrer's Face

from the **WALT DISNEY MOTION PICTURE**

©1942
DISNEY

BUY WAR BONDS
AND STAMPS
FOR VICTORY

ords and Music by
LIVER WALLACE

SOUTHERN MUSIC
PUBLISHING CO., INC.
1619 BROADWAY, NEW YORK

A defaced portrait of Mussolini hangs on a tree in 1944.

CHAPTER 21

THE AXIS IN RETREAT

Hitler and Mussolini won many victories in the war's early years. By 1943, the tide was turning.

IF THERE WAS A WEAK LINK IN THE AXIS CHAIN, it was Italy. The Italian people eventually became weary of war and the loss of military and civilian lives. They blamed it all on their leader, <u>Mussolini</u>. In July 1943, the Allied forces began an invasion of Italy. Troops landed on the island of Sicily to the south and took it by mid-August. Mussolini was forced to resign and was imprisoned by his own people. Six weeks later, he was rescued by German troops and moved to safety in northern Italy.

Meanwhile, the Allied troops were pushing their way through the countryside toward Rome. They were now fighting mostly German soldiers who had been sent by Hitler to save Italy. But Hitler could not protect Mussolini. On April 27, 1945, Mussolini was traveling with a group of other Fascist leaders when he was recognized by **partisan** fighters at a road blockade. The next day, Mussolini was stood up against a wall and shot. By the time victorious American troops entered Rome, Milan, and other cities, Italians were thrilled to see them. Many stuck flowers into the soldiers' gun barrels and the guns of their tanks.

Mussolini was known as *il Duce*, which is Italian for "the Leader."

Crowds line the streets of Milan, Italy, to greet U.S. troops in April 1945.

A German tank: Tanks played an important role in the strategies of the war's military leaders.

CHAPTER 22

TOP GENERALS

The Allies' top generals were a gallery of colorful characters. It took a steady hand to control them.

GREAT GENERALS OFTEN HAVE GREAT egos, and World War II's military leaders were no exception. American Douglas MacArthur, supreme commander of Allied forces in the southwest Pacific, was an arrogant man who wore sunglasses and smoked a corncob pipe. Forced to leave his headquarters in the Philippines in March 1942 as the Japanese invaded, MacArthur vowed "I shall return." Three years later, he fulfilled his promise in triumph.

Bernard L. Montgomery, British hero of the Battle of El Alamein in Egypt, was another top general with a huge ego. He was a strict military man who was tough on his officers but inspired the troops he led. Monty, as he was affectionately nicknamed by his men, was constantly trying to get the best of general **Dwight D. Eisenhower**. He was envious of Eisenhower, who was named supreme commander of the Allied forces by President Roosevelt in 1943. Ike, as Eisenhower was called, was coolheaded, restrained, and able to get along with all the Allied leaders, even Monty.

General MacArthur's trademark sunglasses and pipe gave him a memorable appearance.

CHAPTER 23

D-DAY

The Allies prepared a massive invasion that
they hoped would end the war in Europe.

I N THE EARLY HOURS OF JUNE 6, 1944, THE invasion of German-held France began. The Allies, under the command of General Eisenhower, launched a **flotilla** of more than 5,000 ships to transport the invasion forces and their equipment across the English Channel to France's Normandy coast. To move them from the **convoy** to the beaches in the face of enemy fire required an additional 5,000 landing craft. It was the largest **amphibious** operation in history.

Allied troops captured some of the beaches quickly. However, Omaha Beach, the central point of the whole landing front, took five days to capture. The hills overlooking the beach had been strongly fortified by the Germans, and many brave Allied soldiers were shot down as they scrambled onto the beach. However, they eventually secured Omaha Beach and drove the Germans back. The Allies advanced north after taking the French port of Cherbourg. By August 21, 2 million Allied troops had landed on the Normandy beaches. On August 25, Allied soldiers marched into Paris to the rousing cheers of the joyful French people.

The Allies suffered 226,386 casualties during the Normandy invasion.

American soldiers disembark from a landing craft during the invasion of Normandy on D-Day.

FEBRUARY 19

*U.S. Marines land on
Iwo Jima in the Pacific.*

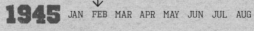

1945 JAN FEB MAR APR MAY JUN JUL AUG

CHAPTER 24

IWO JIMA

The Americans landed on one Pacific island after another in an attempt to reach Japan.

The United States controlled Iwo Jima from 1945 to 1968, when it returned the island to Japan.

I N THE PACIFIC, THE U.S. MILITARY WORKED on a strategy of taking one island at a time on its way to the Japanese mainland. But the Japanese fought hard to hold on to the islands they occupied. Japanese suicide pilots called kamikazes deliberately crashed their planes into attacking Allied ships and aircraft carriers, spreading fear among their crews. Japanese soldiers on the ground were just as fierce in combat. They particularly didn't want to lose the island of Iwo Jima, which lay just 750 miles (1,207 km) from Tokyo, the Japanese capital.

For seven months, American soldiers shelled the island almost daily. Then on February 19, 1945, the Marines landed on the island. The Japanese had carved 1,500 underground rooms connected by 16 miles (26 km) of tunnels in the island's hard volcanic rock. From there, they fought the Americans to the last man. Many American troops died in the tunnels. But enough Marines got through to make a final assault up Mount Suribachi, where the Japanese remained entrenched. With bullets whizzing around them, five American servicemen hoisted the American flag, signaling that they had taken the island.

The image of soldiers raising the American flag on Iwo Jima is one of the most famous images of the entire war.

The V-1 rocket was one of Germany's most destructive weapons during the war.

CHAPTER 25

ROCKETS OF WAR

Germany was losing the war, but it had a secret weapon in store.

GERMANY'S SECRET WEAPON WAS THE V-1 rocket. The V stood for *vergeltung*, "vengeance" in German. A guided missile filled with explosives, the V-1 was cheaper to make than bomber planes and didn't need a human pilot. Beginning in June 1944, shortly after the D-Day invasion, V-1 rockets were launched over Great Britain and Belgium. The bombardment went on for nine months. Only about a quarter of the rockets hit their targets, but they destroyed thousands of buildings and killed more than 6,000 people. The V-1 made a whistling sound before it struck, which served as a warning for the intended victims to run for the cover of a building or air-raid shelter.

In September 1944, German scientists developed an even deadlier rocket, the V-2. It was much bigger than the V-1, packed more explosives, and was far more accurate. Hitler ordered his new "wonder weapon" dropped on Britain and <u>Belgium</u>. But while 9,000 V-2s were launched and caused considerable damage to the Allies, the attacks were too late to save Germany.

Hitler chose Antwerp, Belgium, for a target because it was a center for Allied activities.

British citizens stand among the wreckage after a V-2 attack on London in 1945.

*A German officer's cap
lies on the floor of the bunker
where Hitler met his end.*

CHAPTER 26

HITLER'S END

The Allies were closing in on Hitler,
but Germany's leader refused to surrender.

ON DECEMBER 16, 1944, THE GERMANS launched a surprise counterattack against the Americans in the Ardennes Forest in Belgium. It was called the Battle of the Bulge, and it engaged more American troops than any other battle of the war. The counterattack held back the Allies for a time, but cost Germany dearly, with 80,000 to 100,000 casualties.

By April 1945, the Allies were closing in on Berlin, the German capital. While other Nazi leaders fled, Hitler and a small group of loyal followers remained in the city in an underground **bunker**. Rather than face the shame of capture, Hitler chose death. On the morning of April 30, he shook hands with his followers and retired with his wife, actress Eva Braun, to their rooms. That afternoon, she took poison and he shot himself. Hitler left behind a shattered nation. Allied forces entered Berlin on May 2. Five days later, the Germans formally signed an unconditional surrender. The war in Europe was over.

Followers burned the bodies of Hitler and Braun in a garden outside the bunker. Their remains were then buried in a shallow hole made by a falling bombshell.

Soviet soldiers raise their flag in Berlin in April 1945.

*The first atomic bomb
was dropped from a plane
called the* Enola Gay.

CHAPTER 27

THE ATOMIC BOMB

PRESIDENT ROOSEVELT DID NOT LIVE TO SEE Germany's downfall. He died suddenly on April 12, 1945. His successor, **President Harry Truman**, had a difficult decision to make. The United States had a powerful new weapon, the atomic bomb, that could be used against Japan to force it to surrender. Alternately, Truman could order a land invasion of Japan, possibly costing hundreds of thousands of American and Japanese lives. <u>He chose the bomb.</u>

On August 6, 1945, a U.S. plane dropped an atomic bomb on the Japanese city of Hiroshima. The entire city disappeared in a great ball of fire. The blast killed at least 78,000 people and leveled every building within 5 miles (8 km). People directly below the blast were killed immediately. Many others died in the coming years from radiation that was released by the explosion. For two days, no word of surrender came from Japanese leaders.

On August 9, a second bomb was dropped on the city of Nagasaki, killing another 40,000 people. Within a week, Japan surrendered.

Truman's decision is still a topic of much debate today.

A mushroom cloud rises above the city of Nagasaki during the explosion of the second atomic bomb, on August 9, 1945.

People celebrate victory over Japan in the streets of New York City in 1945.

CHAPTER 28

CELEBRATING THE WAR'S END

The war was over, and much of the
world was ready to celebrate.

AUGUST 14, 1945, V-J (VICTORY OVER JAPAN) Day, was a cause for joy worldwide. People across the globe left their jobs and gathered in the streets. Strangers talked, laughed, kissed, and danced. <u>New York City's</u> Times Square was more crowded than it was on a typical New Year's Eve.

There were also celebrations in many other cities, from London to Manila in the Philippines. The war was over, and many people were just grateful to be alive. These included the thousands of survivors of the Nazi concentration camps who were liberated in the closing days of the war in Europe. Afraid to return to their former homes, many survivors migrated westward to other European countries. Some later moved farther to such countries as the United States, Canada, Australia, and Israel.

In New York City's Garment District, workers threw ticker tape and scraps of cloth out of windows that left a pile 5 inches (13 centimeters) deep in the streets.

Photographer Alfred Eisenstaedt's shot of two people kissing during V-J Day celebrations is one of the most iconic images of the war.

Prisoners at the Dachau
concentration camp cheer as
Allied forces set them free in 1945.

CHAPTER 29

JUDGMENT AT NUREMBERG

Some of Germany's leaders survived the war. Those captured had to face judgment for their war crimes.

THE LIBERATION OF THE CONCENTRATION camps by Allied soldiers at war's end stunned the world. For the first time, people saw the countless dead bodies and the survivors who resembled living skeletons. Camp guards were forced by the Allies to bury the bodies of the dead. A greater punishment awaited the men who planned and operated the death camps or were guilty of other war crimes.

On November 20, 1945, 21 Nazi leaders were put on trial. The trial was held in Nuremberg, the former site of Nazi Party war rallies, in one of the few buildings left standing after Allied bombing. The evidence shown in court included films made of the death camps and tearful eyewitness accounts from camp survivors. The trial lasted 10 months. It ended with 12 defendants receiving death sentences, 7 receiving prison sentences, and 3 being acquitted.

One of the generals who was sentenced to death was Hermann Goering, Hitler's second-in-command. Two hours before his execution, he killed himself with cyanide poison. In addition to the Germans, many Japanese military leaders were also tried and convicted of war crimes.

Goering hid the cyanide in a copper cartridge shell.

Hermann Goering, Hitler's second-in-command, stands trial in Nuremberg in 1946.

CHAPTER 30

EUROPE REBORN

Europe lay in ruins. Would the victors make the
same mistakes they did after World War I?

Marshall was a leading general in World War II and later served in the Truman administration, first as secretary of state and then as secretary of defense.

WORLD WAR II WAS THE MOST destructive war in history. Some historians estimate the total death count to be as high as 55 million. Europe was left broken by six long years of fighting. U.S. secretary of state George Marshall devised a plan to rebuild it. The Marshall Plan distributed $13.5 billion in American aid to 18 European countries from 1948 to 1952. The largest share went to Great Britain and France, but Germany and Italy also received funds.

The Soviet Union had seized power in many Eastern European countries after the war. It also took over eastern Germany, while the other Allies occupied the western portion. Berlin was divided into four sectors—three controlled by the Western Allies (the United States, Great Britain, and France) and the fourth by the Soviets. West Germany was eventually given its independence, while East Germany remained under Soviet control. By 1947, these developments had led to a different kind of war between the United States and the Soviet Union—a Cold War that would last for more than four decades.

German women clean up debris from bombings in Berlin in 1945.

President Franklin D. Roosevelt (1933–45) of the United States was elected during the Great Depression, which he helped end. His programs put Americans to work again and restored the economy. In 1939, Roosevelt faced a new challenge—a war in Europe that many Americans wanted to stay out of.

President Harry S. Truman (1945–53) of the United States was thrust into the presidency upon Roosevelt's death. During the final days of the war, he had to make a tough decision about whether to use nuclear bombs on Japan.

General Dwight D. Eisenhower was one of the leading Allied military leaders of the war. He planned and led the D-Day invasion of France on June 6, 1944. A popular war hero, Eisenhower succeeded Truman as president in 1953 and served two terms.

Prime Minister Winston Churchill of Great Britain came into office shortly before the war began. He quickly proved a determined leader in a war that would consume not only Europe but the entire world.

Joseph Stalin had been leader of the Soviet Union for 10 years when World War II began. A ruthless dictator, he switched sides during the war when he found his country under attack by Germany.

Adolf Hitler of Germany promised the German people that he would make their nation great again. He claimed that the Aryan race of white, northern Europeans had the right to rule and persecute non-Aryans, especially Jews and other minorities. It was Hitler's lust for power that led the world to war.

Benito Mussolini of Italy was a dictator who took control of Italy in the years before Hitler's similar rise in Germany. The two power-hungry leaders joined forces to try to conquer Europe and Africa and create their own empires.

Hideki Tojo of Japan began his career as one of a number of Japanese military leaders who wanted to conquer mainland Asia and build an empire. He gradually emerged as Japan's top military leader, and for much of the war he served as his nation's prime minister.

WORLD WAR II TIMELINE

SEPTEMBER 1
Germany invades and swiftly conquers Poland.

OCTOBER 30
Unable to break British resistance, Hitler ends the bombing and calls off the invasion.

JUNE 22
France surrenders to Germany.

1939 JAN FEB MAR APR MAY JUN JUL AUG **SEP** OCT NOV DEC **1940** JAN FEB MAR APR MAY **JUN JUL** AUG SEP **OCT** NOV

SEPTEMBER 3
Great Britain and France declare war on Germany; World War II begins.

JULY
Germany begins a massive bombing campaign against Great Britain, with plans for a land invasion.

JUNE 22
Germany begins its surprise invasion of the Soviet Union.

OCTOBER 23
Allied forces defeat the Germans at the Battle of El Alamein in North Africa.

DECEMBER 8
The United States declares war on Japan.

1941 JAN FEB MAR APR MAY **JUN** JUL AUG SEP OCT NOV **DEC** **1942** JAN FEB MAR APR MAY **JUN** JUL AUG SEP **OCT** NOV DEC

JUNE 4–6
The Americans defeat the Japanese at the Battle of Midway in the Pacific.

DECEMBER 7
The Japanese launch a sneak attack on the American fleet at Pearl Harbor in Hawaii.

WORLD WAR II TIMELINE

JANUARY 31
*The Soviets defeat
Germany at the Battle
of Stalingrad.*

JUNE 6
*D-Day, the Allied
invasion of Normandy on
the French coast, begins.*

1943 JAN FEB MAR APR MAY JUN **JUL** AUG SEP OCT NOV DEC **1944** JAN FEB MAR APR MAY **JUN** JUL **AUG** SEP OCT NOV

JULY
*The Allied invasion
of Italy begins.*

AUGUST 25
*Allied troops liberate
German-occupied Paris.*

DECEMBER 16
*The Battle of the Bulge
begins in Belgium's
Ardennes Forest.*

FEBRUARY 19
U.S. Marines land on
Iwo Jima in the Pacific.

AUGUST 6
The United States drops
an atomic bomb on the
Japanese city of Hiroshima,
killing and maiming many
thousands of people.

APRIL 30
Hitler shoots himself
in a Berlin bunker to
escape capture.

NOVEMBER 20
The trial of Nazi war
criminals begins in
Nuremberg, Germany.

945   JAN FEB MAR APR MAY JUN JUL AUG SEP OCT NOV DEC   **1946 1947 1948**

APRIL 28
Italian dictator Benito
Mussolini is killed by
partisan forces.

SEPTEMBER 2
The official surrender
ceremony takes
place aboard the
USS Missouri, and
World War II ends.

1948
The Marshall Plan
begins to distribute
$13.5 billion
in aid to help
rebuild Europe.

AUGUST 9
An atomic bomb is dropped
on Nagasaki, Japan. Six
days later, on August 14, the
Japanese surrender.

GLOSSARY

- **alliance** (uh-LYE-uhns) an agreement to work together for some result

- **amphibious** (am-FIB-ee-us) relating to a military operation that combines land and water

- **appeasement** (uh-PEEZ-muhnt) the process of making someone content or calm to avoid conflict

- **armada** (ahr-MAH-duh) a large group of warships

- **armaments** (AHR-muh-muhnts) weapons and other equipment used for fighting wars

- **armistice** (AHR-muh-stus) a temporary agreement to stop a war

- **black market** (BLAK MAR-kit) an economy where goods are bought and sold illegally

- **bunker** (BUHNG-kur) an underground shelter

- **convoy** (KAHN-voi) a group of vehicles or ships that travel together for convenience or safety

- **demilitarized** (dee-MIL-uh-tuh-rized) cleared of military presence and placed under civil control

- **dictators** (DIK-tay-turz) rulers who have complete control of a country, often by force

- **drafted** (DRAF-tid) required to serve in a country's armed forces

- **fascist** (FASH-ist) relating to a form of government in which a dictator and the dictator's political party have complete control over a country

- **flotilla** (flo-TIL-uh) a group of small naval ships

- **ghettos** (GET-ohz) poor neighborhoods in a city where people of the same race, religion, or ethnic background live by choice or by force

- **isolationists** (eye-suh-LAY-shuhn-ists) people who believe in the policy of keeping a country from participating in foreign affairs

- **munitions** (myoo-NISH-uhnz) weapons and ammunition

- **neutral** (NOO-truhl) not supporting or agreeing with either side of a disagreement or competition

- **partisan** (PART-uz-un) a member of a military group fighting against an occupying army

- **propaganda** (prah-puh-GAN-duh) information that is spread to influence the way people think, to gain supporters, or to damage an opposing group

- **rationed** (RASH-uhnd) distributed in limited amounts

- **siege** (SEEJ) the surrounding of a place such as a castle or city to cut off supplies and then wait for those inside to surrender

- **snipers** (SNIPE-urz) soldiers who fire at enemy soldiers from a distant, concealed location

- **theater** (THEE-uh-tur) an area where military operations take place

FIND OUT MORE

BOOKS

Atwood, Kathryn J. *Women Heroes of World War II*. Chicago: Chicago Review Press, 2011.

Frank, Anne. *Anne Frank: The Diary of a Young Girl*. New York: Bantam, 1993 [reprint].

Hillenbrand, Laura. *Unbroken: An Olympian's Journey from Airman to Castaway to Capture*. New York: Delacorte, 2014.

Mailer, Norman. *The Naked and the Dead*. New York: Picador, 2000 [50th anniversary edition].

FILMS

Cartoons for Victory! (1940s). DVD, Mackinac Media, 2006.

The Great Dictator (1940). DVD, Criterion Collection, 2011.

Saving Private Ryan (1998). DVD, Dreamworks Video, 1999.

Schindler's List (1993). Universal Studios Home Entertainment, 2013.

NOTE: Some books and films may not be appropriate for younger viewers.

VISIT THIS SCHOLASTIC WEB SITE FOR
MORE INFORMATION ABOUT **WORLD WAR II**
www.factsfornow.scholastic.com
WORLD WAR II

INDEX

Page numbers in *italics* indicate illustrations.

ABOUT THE AUTHOR

Steven Otfinoski has written more than 180 books for young readers. They include books about Pearl Harbor, D-Day, and the Hump Airmen. Three of his books have been named to the New York Public Library's list of recommendations, Books for the Teen Age. He lives with his family in Connecticut.